TATE CREATE: THINGS TO MAKE & DO BY ARTISTS

Edited by Sally Tallant

Things to Make

Things to Do

How to use this book

Welcome to this amazing book, which is packed full of ideas and activities by leading international artists. Each of them has created something for you to make or do, whatever your age. Some of the activities can be done on your own and some of them are designed for trying out with other people. Activities include drawing, collage, cooking and eating, meditating, looking, thinking, asking questions and working things out. It is an art school in a book.

I love making things and have done since I was a child, and I have been lucky that I am able to work with artists every day. The artists in this book all make art in different styles and we hope their activities show that there are many ways to look at the world and help you find your own methods to make and think about art.

The artists have all been asked the following five questions that will give you an insight to why they became artists:

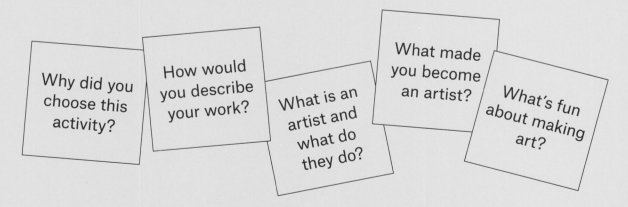

Why did you choose this activity?

How would you describe your work?

What is an artist and what do they do?

What made you become an artist?

What's fun about making art?

Once you have finished all of the activities in the book you can answer them yourself.

Sally Tallant

Amalia Pica

Create absurd creatures

Have you noticed that there are sometimes pictures hidden in the way we talk? Most languages use expressions such as the 'neck of a bottle', 'head of broccoli' or the 'tongue of a shoe'. They don't sound funny to say, but seeing them is different. Amalia Pica was born in Argentina but is now based in London. Try her Surrealist exercise for transforming words into pictures.

You will need:

Copier, scanner or printer
Paper or card
Scissors
PVA (craft) glue

Optional: cut-outs from photographs, magazines or images found online

1
To make your absurd creatures, copy the following pages and cut out the items. These are your body parts. You can also draw in details or add photographs of your own.

2
Combine the body parts in weird and wonderful ways. Then stick them down on card. You could even make your new friends stand up by adding a triangle at the back like a picture frame.

Why did you choose this activity?
I think sometimes art helps us to pay attention. Often we say things that are quite absurd and it is easier to notice them when we can look at what we say.

What is an artist and what do they do?
Artists are normal people who have an amazingly fun job, but making art and thinking of ideas can sometimes be hard too.

What made you become an artist?
I was scared at first because I also liked reading and was good at school (yes, I was a nerd), and I worried that focusing on making art would not allow me to develop other skills. I soon found out that art can be whatever you want it to be, so reading and thinking also became part of my artwork.

How would you describe your work?
Artworks are very hard to describe, that is why they need to exist, and for them to exist we need to make them!

What's fun about making art?
I like starting something from scratch and once I am done, thinking, 'Hey, this didn't exist a few hours ago!' It is a bit like magic.

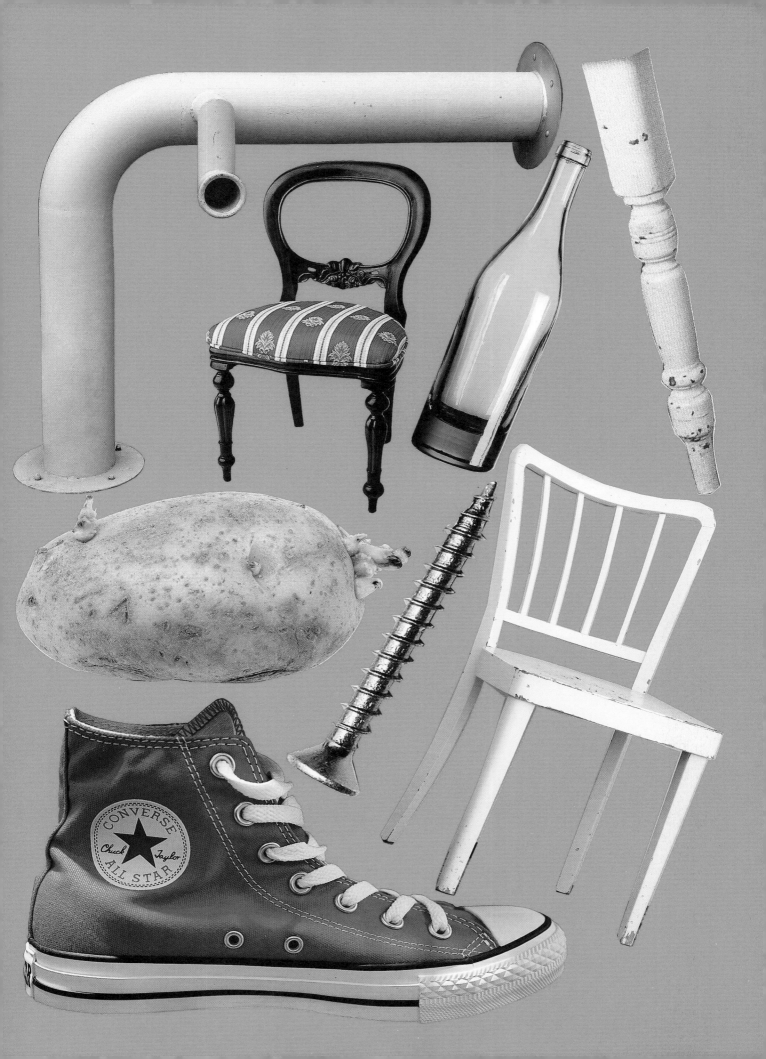

David Shrigley

Make your mark

David Shrigley is a British conceptual artist. His witty drawings and sculptures are instantly recognisable for their whimsical style, their deliberate simplicity undercut by his deadpan worldview. A fan of basic printing techniques, here he instructs you to make a handprint but call it a footprint. Why? It makes you do a double take, and makes you think about art as being about ideas, not just images. And it's just plain silly. Like life.

You will need:

Paint
Paper
A hand

Why did you choose this activity?
I like doing it and I have been doing this a long time and I am very good at it.

What is an artist and what do they do?
I can only speak for myself, not for all artists, but I would say this: a successful artist is a very lucky person who does not have a proper job and can do whatever they like all day (as long as it is making art).

What made you become an artist?
At first I wanted to become an astronaut but that was not possible as I am too big to fit in a spaceship. Then I decided to be a professional footballer but that was also not possible because my feet are too big. So then I decided to be an artist because you can do that regardless of how big you are.

How would you describe your work?
My work is about everything in the world. Sometimes it is funny and sometimes it isn't.

What's fun about making art?
Making art is fun because it flexes the creative muscles in your brain and that makes you happy.

FOOTPRINT

Linder

Make a salad portrait

Linder is a British artist – her radical style of photomontage combines images from magazines with other archival material. Her work makes us question the images that advertising puts in front of us. Recently she has started to make 'living' collages. Here she shows you how to become an artwork using salad ingredients.

Thank you to my models Rowan, Orban, Vita and Amira!

You will need:

Scissors
Images of eyes and mouths
A selection of salad
ingredients and vegetables
Lots of fresh herbs
Knife
Camera

Optional: fabric to lie on
(a sheet, towel or tablecloth)

Artist's Note

If you want to take a selfie make sure everything you need will be in easy reach (including a camera or phone) before you lie-down! Arrange the salad ingredients around you and on your face, then add the cut-outs. Very carefully reach for the camera and take photos of yourself.

Why did you choose this activity?
I chose to make a living collage because it's a new way of making images for me – normally I use cut-outs from magazines to make pictures. More recently I've started to make collages in front of the camera with objects and dancers; it's a very exciting way to work because the unexpected can happen at any moment!

What is an artist and what do they do?
Often, when I tell people that I'm an artist, they ask me if I paint or draw. I always explain that I rarely paint or draw, that I choose to work with photographs instead. Each artist is different and that's the joy of it all – we can't be pinned down.

What made you become an artist?
As a child, I would always draw pictures of imaginary people in imaginary worlds; art was my escape route from the everyday. In some ways it still is, art allows freedom of expression, which is something that everyone needs. Artists get more than their fair share of free expression though, we're very lucky.

How would you describe your work?
I stick things together that don't normally go together so that new meanings can emerge. I work with the techniques of collage within photography, dance, costume and music – it's an endlessly fascinating way of reconfiguring the world that I see around me. If I'm working purely with photographs then the technique is called photomontage, everything else falls under the umbrella of collage.

What's fun about making art?
There aren't any rules! There are traditions and techniques galore within the history of art but artists are always questioning the past and always searching for newness in the present. We're often trying to say and express that which can't be said by words alone. Sometimes we're misunderstood but that all adds to the fun and unpredictability of what we do!

1
Cut out pictures of eyes and mouths from magazines and newspapers or print images that you find online. Collect a variety of lip shades and eye shapes.

2
Gather together your salad ingredients. Make sure you have enough to decorate on and around someone's whole head.

3
Cut colourful vegetables – such as bell peppers, carrots or cucumbers – into different shapes and sizes. Use cherry tomatoes whole.

4
To make the portraits you can work indoors or outdoors. You could place your subjects on a sheet, textile or tablecloth so that it's easy to clean up afterwards. The fabric will be in the photo, so you might want to choose something colourful or with a pattern.

5
Arrange the salad ingredients around and on top of the participants' faces. Use different colours and textures of vegetables to make your portraits as varied as possible.

Artist's Note

If you're going to photograph a few people, make sure that they have their heads close together (ideally touching) so that they will all fit into the photograph. Make sure to leave enough room between their bodies so that you can step very close to their heads. You are going to be photographing them directly from above.

6
Add the pictures of eyes and mouths at the end – you can have lots of fun with this, the final effect should look quite strange. Try placing a cut-out of an eye over someone's real eye or lips over their lips. Or put an eye on the palm of a hand.

Olafur Eliasson

Eating with your ears

Food is very important to Icelandic-Danish artist Olafur Eliasson. Most days at his studio in Berlin his team sits down together to share lunch and exchange ideas. The organic, vegetarian meals are prepared by a team of cooks in his studio kitchen, who also prepared these recipes for you. With this cooking and listening activity he wants you to think about how eating connects us to our bodies and to the physical world around us.

Sound Experiment

Use two cups to cover your ears. What do you hear? Is there a low rumbling sound like a distant ocean? You can alter the sound by changing the distance between them and your ears, and by changing the angle at which you hold them. Sounds from all around you get caught in the cups, bounce around inside and get mixed into a single sound – just like the ingredients you are going to use in these recipes get mixed into one dish.

Sound Experiment

While you eat the food you've cooked, cover your ears with your hands. What do you hear? The sounds the food makes when you chew it usually flow out of your ears – but when you block your ears, the sounds stay inside and you can hear them clearly. What do the different foods sound like?

Why did you choose this activity?
The ingredients of a meal connect us to the environment and to nature, and the actions of cooking and eating food can help us to be more aware of our bodies, our perceptions and our feelings. Art starts with taking an interest in our experience of the world, with being curious about our experiences, as well as about where things come from and how they are made.

What is an artist and what do they do?
Like everyone, no matter what their job might be, an artist is someone whose activities help to make and to change the world that we all live in together.

What made you become an artist?
When I was young, I liked shaping things. Even though it took me a while to learn to draw, I was excited about colours and imagination. Sometimes I made abstract

drawings that did not look like anything at first, but then I imagined what they were: they could be a cat or a volcano! So I started liking things that were abstract, things that could mean many things – and I realised that art is like that.

How would you describe your work?
My work would like to know what you think about it. My work is interested in how you see it and how you feel it. Also, later on, my work wants to know if you still remember what it felt like.

What's fun about making art?
For me making art is like shaping the world. When I make a sculpture, I change the way the world looks – even if it's at a very small scale. I like that art and the world are connected. Through my art I feel close to the world.

Crisp bread

1

Mix the salt and flour together in a bowl. If using active dry yeast, stir it into the flour with the sugar.

2

In another bowl, mix together the fresh yeast (if using), sugar and warm water. Let the mixture rest for 15 minutes, until the yeast has activated and bubbled up.

3

Next, carefully pour the wet ingredients into the dry ones, mix well and knead the mixture until it forms a ball.

4

Place the ball in a clean bowl and cover with a clean cloth. Let the dough rise in a warm place for at least 30 minutes.

Ingredients:

(Serves six)

1 teaspoon salt
500 g plain/4 cups all purpose flour
20 g/¾ oz fresh yeast
or 1½ teaspoons active dry yeast
1 teaspoon sugar
300 ml/1⅓ fl oz warm water
Fresh herbs, such as coriander (cilantro), chives or parsley
Olive oil
Seeds or spices, such as white or black sesame seeds, sunflower seeds, pumpkin seeds or pink peppercorns
Coarse sea salt

Equipment

2 mixing bowls
A clean cloth
Pastry brush
Baking parchment

5

During this time, you can prepare the herbs – wash and dry them, and pluck off the leaves.

6

Set the oven at 175°C/350°F/gas mark 3.

7

To make one large crisp bread, roll out the dough on a sheet of baking parchment. It should be as thin as possible, so thin that you can almost see through it. If you want to make smaller crisp breads, divide the dough into quarters before rolling it out on the baking parchment.

8

Brush the flattened dough with olive oil.

9

Decorate the dough with the herbs or the seeds – or both! In the photos we have done the herbs and seeds separately but you can do it however you like.

10

Cover the dough with another sheet of parchment and roll again, so that the herbs and seeds are pressed flat into it.

11

Sprinkle the dough with the coarse sea salt, then bake it. Put it in the oven for 10–12 minutes – depending on how thin the dough is. Check regularly. It will look crisp around the edges and golden-brown when it is ready.

Enjoy your bread with the pink labneh (page 22) and pickled carrots (page 24).

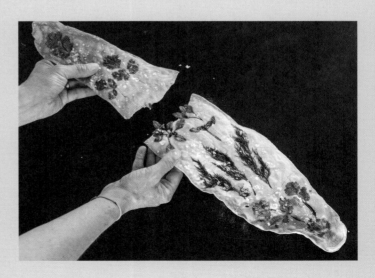

Pink labneh

1

Line a colander with cheesecloth, then place it in a large bowl.

2

In another bowl, combine the puréed beetroot, yogurt and 1½ teaspoons salt. Mix well.

3

Spoon the mixture into the colander and then cover with a lid or clean cloth and place it in the refrigerator for 4 hours or overnight – the longer the yogurt drains, the more firm it becomes. You can check periodically to see how it changes.

Ingredients:

(Serves six)

One cooked red beetroot (beet), puréed
400 g/1¼ cups Greek
or Turkish full-fat yogurt
Olive oil
Salt and pepper

To garnish:
fresh thyme,
roasted sesame seeds,
lemon zest and sumac

Equipment

Colander
Cheesecloth
Large bowl
2x medium-sized bowl
Clean lid or cloth
Serving bowl

4

Transfer the mixture into a bowl and stir in a bit of olive oil. Taste to see if it needs salt and pepper, then mix some of them in too – as little or as much as you like.

5

Put it into a pretty serving bowl and sprinkle it with thyme, sesame seeds, lemon zest and sumac.

Pickled carrots

1
Arrange the carrot spears
nicely in the glass jar and add
the spices and garlic.

2
Pour the vinegar, water and honey
into a pan over medium heat, and stir
until the honey has dissolved.

3
Let the mixture cool for a minute or two,
then pour it over the carrots.

4
Let everything cool completely, then cover
and place in the refrigerator for one or two
nights – or for as long as a fortnight.

5
Every day or two, you can open the jar and
taste the carrots to see how the flavour
and texture develop over time. This recipe
also works well with cucumbers, radishes,
kohlrabi, summer squash and other firm
vegetables – and experimenting with
adding fresh herbs and different spices
is a lot of fun too.

Ingredients:

(Makes one 500 ml/16 fl oz jar)

4 medium-sized carrots,
peeled and cut into spears
1 bay leaf
1 teaspoon mustard seeds
2 small chilli peppers
2 cloves of garlic
150 ml/5 fl oz white balsamic vinegar
75 ml/2½ fl oz water
75 ml/2½ fl oz honey

Equipment

Glass jar with a lid
Pan for heating

Artist's Note

Where possible, I encourage you to
use organic ingredients and to buy
them at shops that are within walking
or cycling distance of your home – you
can include the journey to get the
ingredients as part of the activity.

Yto Barrada

Make your own damn pink!

Moroccan born, New York-based artist Yto Barrada wants you to get some colour into your life and to 'make your own damn pink!' Here she shares her simple introduction to natural dyeing using things you already have in your kitchen. You'll soon be in the pink.

Illustrations by Yto's daughter, Vega Gullette, thank you!

You will need:

Knife
Skins and stones (pits) from 6–8 avocados
2 large pans (one with a lid)
Strainer
Tongs or wooden spoon
White fabric (t-shirt, dress, pillowcase, try whatever you fancy, natural fibres such as silk, cotton and linen will work best)

Optional: freezer bags
Rubber gloves
Pickling lime

Why did you choose this activity?
I like this activity because it is easy – and it is magic! Marvel as the stones (pits) and skins of the friendly guacamole fruit transform into a dye with tones of rose, fuchsia and coral.

What is an artist and what do they do?
An artist is a maker of things and sometimes a creator of ideas. Recently, I have started making my own dyes from plant seeds, foraged flowers and bark. It has been so much fun.

What made you become an artist?
It was a reaction to the things, places and events around me. I thought I could take a picture and describe what I saw and share it.

How would you describe your work?
First, I would say I create images – often photographs but also drawings and posters too. I also make sculpture. Detail, colour and scale all matter to me. My work is serious, I like to explore subjects linked to history and geography, but it can be playful too. For example, I have made oversized toys to explore geology. Often it is about Morocco where I grew up and still have a house.

What's fun about making art?
Working with people to transform ideas into things.

Note: Pickling lime is used in this activity as an optional fixative. It can be easily sourced online, but be sure to always use a product of 'food grade' quality and to follow label instructions carefully. Use with caution if anyone has allergies and always supervise children.

1
Halve and remove the stones (pits) from the avocados and scrape as much of the green flesh away from the skins and stones as you can. You won't need to use the flesh for this activity. Chop up the skins.

2
Let the skins and stones dry on your window if it's a sunny day or freeze them in a freezer bag. If you don't want to eat or cook with 6–8 avocados all at once, you can put your skins and stones aside in the freezer until you are ready for dyeing day.

3
When you are ready to begin dyeing, fill a large pan (approx. 20 cm/8 in diameter, best to use one you don't cook with) about half-full with water. Add the stones and skins and place on a medium heat. Don't allow it to boil. After around 15 minutes the water will begin to turn pink. The longer you leave it to simmer the deeper the colour will become; after around 45 minutes you will get a deep maroon.

4
Remove from the heat and very carefully strain your dye into the second pan to remove the avocado pieces. It's OK if it cools off a little bit before you start dyeing.

5
Soak your fabric in cold water, then remove and wring out the excess (set aside the water for step 7 if you are using pickling lime). Add your fabric to the dye with tongs or a wooden spoon.

6
Steep your fabric in the dye. Turn it often to distribute the colour evenly. Use utensils that are dye-resistant or that you don't mind becoming a little pink (such as a wooden spoon). The longer you leave it the more intense the colour becomes. Check how it develops every couple of hours and remove the fabric when you like the colour.

7
If using pickling lime, put on rubber gloves and add a heaped tablespoon to the water you reserved in step 5, stir well. Soak your fabric in the solution for ten minutes. This will make your colours brighter and last longer. Then rinse the fabric in cold, running water until the water runs clear. (If not using pickling lime you can move straight to rinsing the fabric.)

8
Hang your fabric up to dry. And then wear your own damn pink with pride!

Artist's Note
Keep experimenting. The pH of your tap water will influence the colour, so try using rain water, filtered water or sea water to achieve different shades of pink, or try varying the amount or ripeness of the avocados you use.

Carlos Cruz-Diez

Discover additive colour

French-Venezuelan artist Carlos Cruz-Diez has been called a 'master of colour' and he is fascinated by the science behind our perception. He often creates artworks that can fool the eye and almost seem to move (known as Kinetic Art). In this sense, his paintings are visual experiences that encourage conversation about the difference between what we perceive and what is real. Here, he invites you to use a fidget spinner to create mysterious 'additive' colours. Get spinning!

You will need:

Copier, scanner or printer
Poster or gouache paint
(ideally red, green and blue)
Paintbrush
Thick paper or card
Scissors
Sticky tape
Fidget spinner

Why did you choose this activity?
In all my work, I like to explore our perception and to create things that are unusual for the brain to interpret. I love that colour is not something fixed but something that happens that is constantly changing. It is something amazing created in the moment by you, the viewer, when you look at my art. I like to use your eyes and how you perceive colour as my paintbrush.

What is an artist and what do they do?
An artist is someone who is born with the desire to discover, to invent and to communicate.

What made you become an artist?
When I was six years old, I received a box of coloured pencils as a gift. That changed my life.

How would you describe your work?
The launching of colour into space... When I was at the School of Fine Arts in Caracas, I liked to think about how earlier artists used colour in their artworks. I noticed that colour was always attached to a 'form', becoming only an adjective to an object, for example: the 'red' apple, the 'yellow' truck. In the nineteenth century, Impressionist artists such as Claude Monet used colour to paint the same landscape at different times of the day, and make obvious the changing nature of light. Other artists used colour for symbolism, to convey meaning. Vincent van Gogh painted his *Sunflowers* almost entirely in yellow, not only to illustrate the radiance of the flowers but also to associate them with the brightness of the sun. The painting was also intended to welcome the arrival of his friend Paul Gauguin at the Yellow House in Arles, France, where Van Gogh lived for a time. While artists have been exploring colour perception for centuries, I realised that colour itself was not the focus. I decided to create art that was purely about colour and that made the viewer's experience of the work integral.

What's fun about making art?
It is a euphoric adventure – an adventure that has no end.

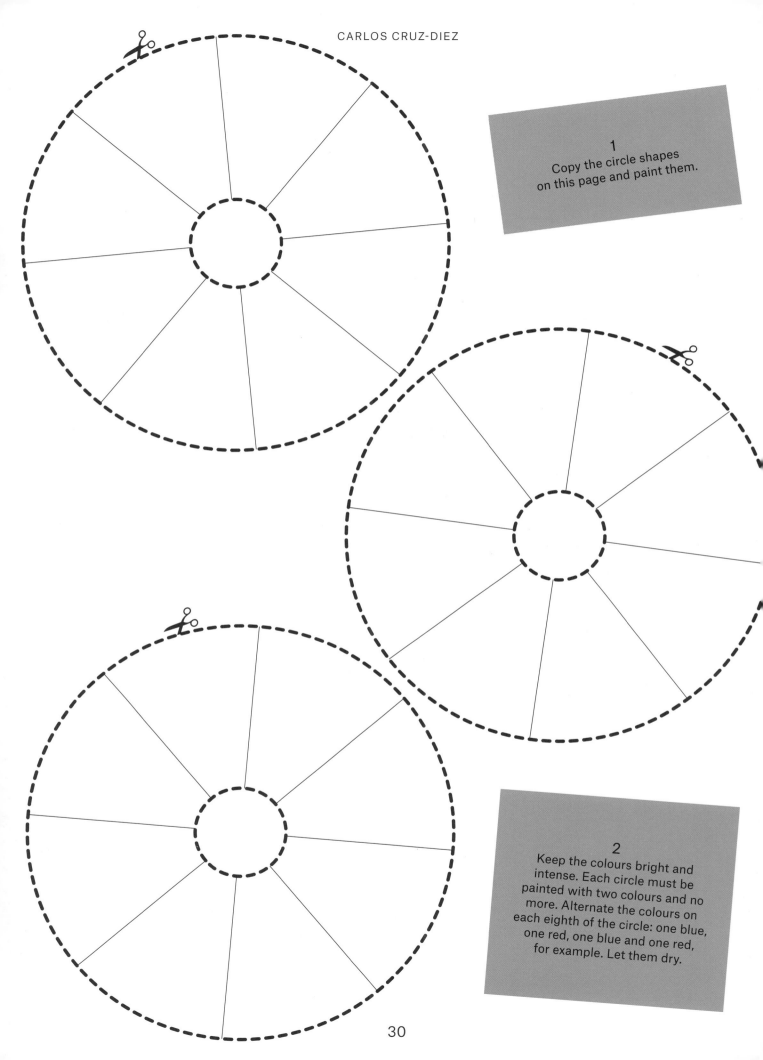

1
Copy the circle shapes on this page and paint them.

2
Keep the colours bright and intense. Each circle must be painted with two colours and no more. Alternate the colours on each eighth of the circle: one blue, one red, one blue and one red, for example. Let them dry.

3
Carefully cut out the coloured circles following the dotted lines.

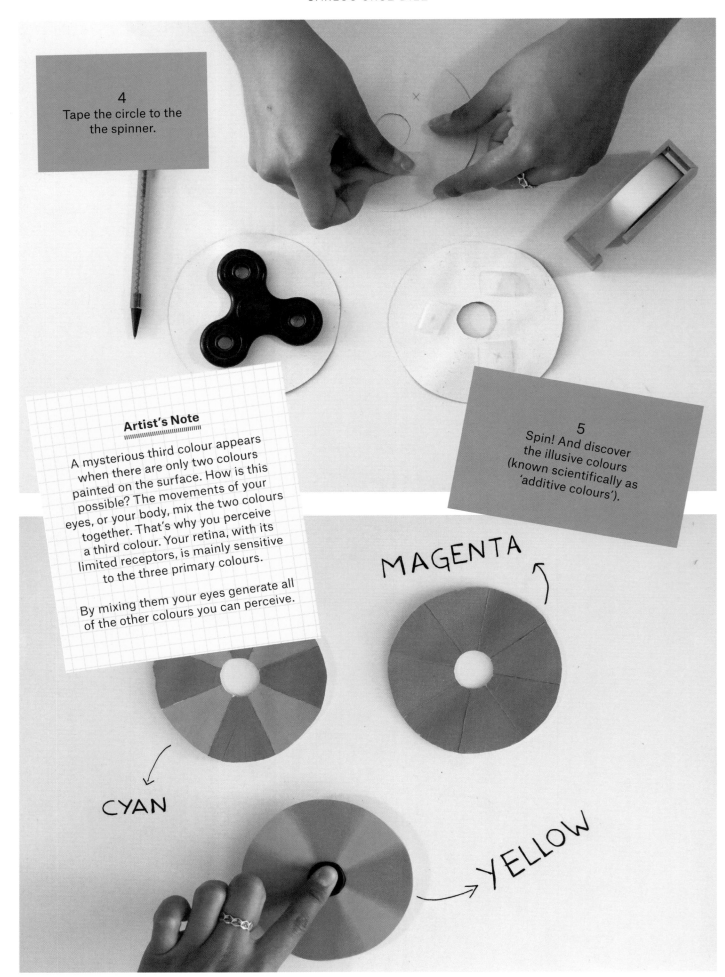

4
Tape the circle to the
the spinner.

Artist's Note

A mysterious third colour appears
when there are only two colours
painted on the surface. How is this
possible? The movements of your
eyes, or your body, mix the two colours
together. That's why you perceive
a third colour. Your retina, with its
limited receptors, is mainly sensitive
to the three primary colours.

By mixing them your eyes generate all
of the other colours you can perceive.

5
Spin! And discover
the illusive colours
(known scientifically as
'additive colours').

MAGENTA

CYAN

YELLOW

Additional Activity

How many colours do you see? Look at this page from far away. Most people will see six: green, red, black, blue, yellow and magenta. If you get closer, do you still see all those colours? Are magenta or yellow really there? These colours are created by the blurring of the colour lines in our brain. We experience them even though they are not painted on the surface.

Carlos Cruz-Diez
Color Aditivo Permutable 1, 2011
Cruz-Diez Art Foundation Collection

Monster Chetwynd

Make a spotted salamander

Monster Chetwynd decided to be an artist so that she could have fun. She was born in London and now lives in Glasgow. She is known for wild performances and elaborate costumes and props that friends and family help her to make. Her work often draws from nature and the fantastical. Here she encourages you to get messy and have fun making a spotted salamander.

You will need:

Cardboard
Scissors
Masking tape
Balloons
Newspaper or scrap materials for stuffing
PVA (craft) glue
Large bowl, bucket or container
Two plastic domes (or round containers/lids)
Black acrylic paint
Paintbrushes
Acrylic or poster paints in bright colours
Kitchen roll

Optional: liquid latex, hairdryer

Why did you choose this activity?
It introduces a lot of different skills within one activity.

What is an artist and what do they do?
An artist is someone who is trained to question the parameters of normality. They should surprise us.

What made you become an artist?
I always wanted to have fun as a child and teenager but on many occasions I was quietly taken aside and told that in life, it is not possible to have fun all the time. As I grew up I understood that there is an allowance to have more fun being an 'artist' than in other walks of life.

How would you describe your work?
Fun.

What's fun about making art?
The diversity, the experimentation, you never know what you're doing – that is a recipe for fun.

Note: Make sure there is adequate ventilation if using latex and follow any manufacturer's instructions with care. Latex is safe for adults and children, but use with caution if anyone has allergies. Always supervise children.

1

To make your salamander's body, first you need to create a frame using cardboard. Thin card or an old cardboard box is best. Flatten out and cut into strips around 2–6 cm (1–2 in) wide. Soften the strips by rubbing them, which makes them easier to bend. The length of the strips depends on how big you want your salamander to be, as a rough guide start with strips around 30 cm (11 in) and shorten as necessary.

2

Start by making the head: bend one strip into a large circle and fasten the ends together with masking tape. This will give you an idea of proportions for the tummy and tail. Once the head shape is made move on to rest of the body. Think of it as if you are drawing with the cardboard. How many circles you need depends on how big you want your salamander to be, try starting with ten. Then join your circles together to make a body shape using strips of cardboard.

3
Next, make four legs for your salamander. Roll two bits of cardboard into tubes and tape together to create an elbow or knee shape. Attach these to your frame using masking tape, two on each side one set closer to the head and the others near the tail.

4
Carefully stuff the head and body with balloons and newspaper (or any paper or stuffing material will do). Remember to put the balloons inside the frame before blowing them up. The stuffing is to support the frame when you cover it in papier-mâché (see step 6).

5
Make a papier-mâché glue by diluting PVA (craft) glue with water in a large bowl, bucket or container. Add the water slowly and stir until the consistency is like pancake batter. (You can use liquid latex instead, which will make your salamander's skin rubbery.)

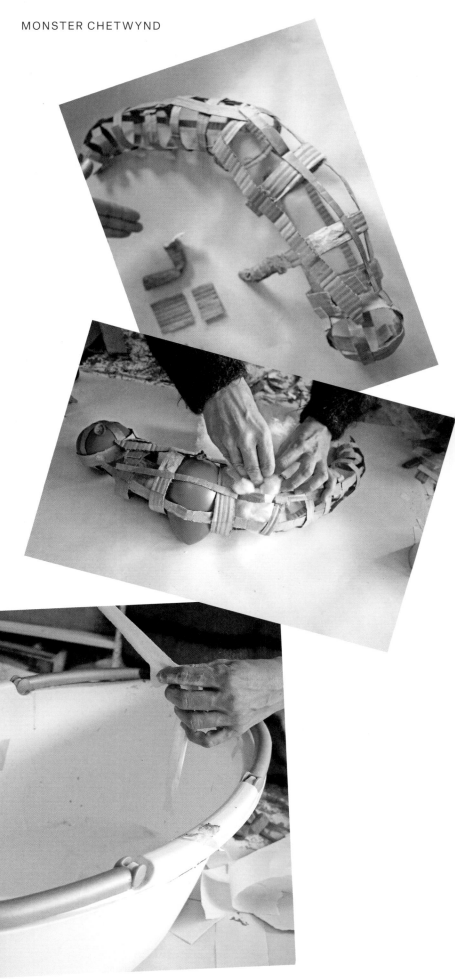

6

Tear the newspaper into strips about 3–4 cm (1–1½ in) wide, then dip them into the papier-mâché glue to coat well. You can wear gloves if you want, but I prefer not to. Wrap the strips around your stuffed frame and make sure all the stuffing and cardboard is covered. Once done, cover and save your paste if you have any left.

7

Set the salamander head and body aside to dry. Leave overnight or at least for a few hours to ensure it is fully dry (the cooler the room the longer it will take). You can speed up the drying time using a hairdryer on a low heat, but be careful to avoid letting the papier-mâché get too hot. (If using latex, check the manufacturer's instructions on drying it safely.)

8

While you wait for the body to dry, make the eyes. You will need two plastic containers or lids that have a nice round shape. You can often buy clear plastic domes from craft shops. These are good because you can paint them on the inside so that they look like glinting eyes. Choose the right size for your salamander. Paint the eyes black.

9
When the body is dry, mix your paint into the leftover papier-mâché glue or, if needed, make a new batch (see step 5). I used red but you can choose any colour.

10
Tear your kitchen roll into strips about 4–5 cm (1½–2 in) in width. Dip them into the paint-glue mixture. Wrap the strips around the head and body of your salamander. (You will only need one layer if using latex.) Have fun covering the whole of the creature – take your time and do it in sections as it will be slippy. You can use a hairdryer on a low heat to help speed up the drying.

11
Wrap the legs and, when they are fully covered, make toes with small pieces of kitchen roll. Cover your paint-glue mixture for later and set aside the salamander for a few more hours to dry.

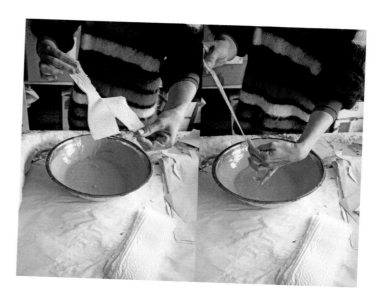

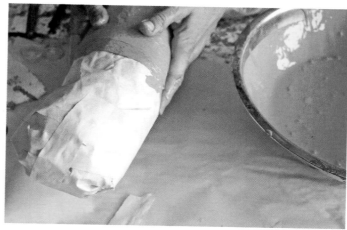

12
Add your salamander's eyes.
Use a little glue, and then secure
them by wrapping strips of kitchen
roll dipped in the paint-glue
mixture around the edges.

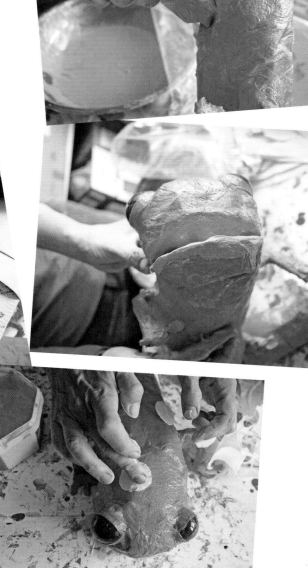

13
Cut a slit around the underside of the head
of the head to make a mouth. Use more
of the paint-glue mixture and some more kitchen
roll to shape and fill in the inside of the mouth.

14
Make another batch of papier-mâché paint-glue
in a different colour for the spots.

15
Cut kitchen roll into circles to make the
spots. Dip the spots into the mix and place
on your salamander. Leave to dry.

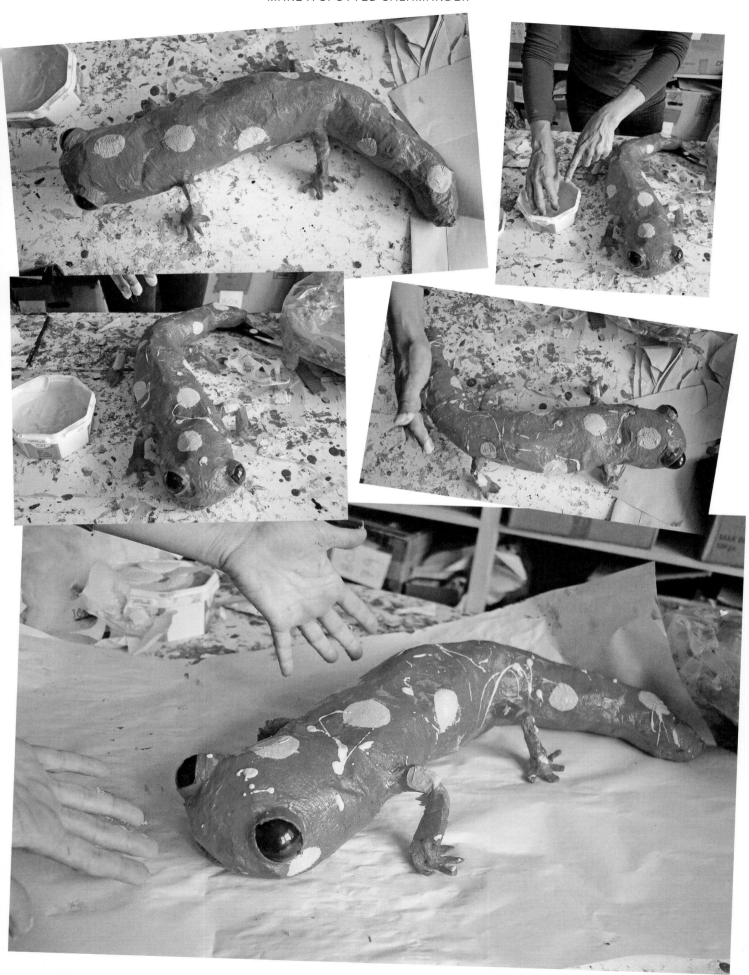

Shezad Dawood

All in the composition

Shezad Dawood is a British artist who likes to 'cut things up' and explore the relationships between them. This exercise demonstrates how to use this cut-up technique to experiment with different compositions. The inspiration comes from an artwork of Dawood's in the Tate collection, which is made of painted panels that can be assembled in any order. Therefore its appearance can change each time it is displayed.

You will need:

Patterned fabric, paper or card
Scissors
Card
PVA (craft) glue
Marker pen
Copier, scanner or printer

Optional: ruler, paint

1

Gather a selection of materials that have different patterns. I've used fabrics, but you could easily use different types of paper or card. Cut them up and arrange them directly onto a copier. Make whatever composition you like. Look at how the patterns work with or against each other and keep rearranging them until you are satisfied.

Why did you choose this activity?
I chose it because it's really close to what I actually do.

What is an artist and what do they do?
An artist is someone who sees the world slightly differently and wants to share the joy that this brings them.

What made you become an artist?
It's all I ever wanted to do. I remember sitting in Tate as a kid and dreaming of my work being there one day.

What's fun about making art?
It's all about cutting things up to see how different patterns and images work together.

How would you describe your work?
You can constantly reimagine the world around you, and get to understand its secrets.

2

When you're ready, print out your composition and glue onto an A4 piece of card.

3

Using a marker pen, draw a 'grid' over your composition, which will guide you when cutting up your designs. You can measure your grid lines with a ruler and space out so that each piece is an equal square (see example on page 44), or you could draw irregular shapes and see the effect that has (see page 45).

4

Cut along the grid lines to create individual squares or shapes. These are the building blocks for your next composition. Rearrange the tiles of the grid to create a new picture. You can do this as much as you like until you are happy with the result.

Artist's Note

If you don't have a copier you can also do this activity by following the same steps as above but instead of arranging your composition on a scanner, glue the patterned pieces directly onto a piece of card.

Additional Activity

Try printing another image on top of your composition before you cut it up and rearrange.

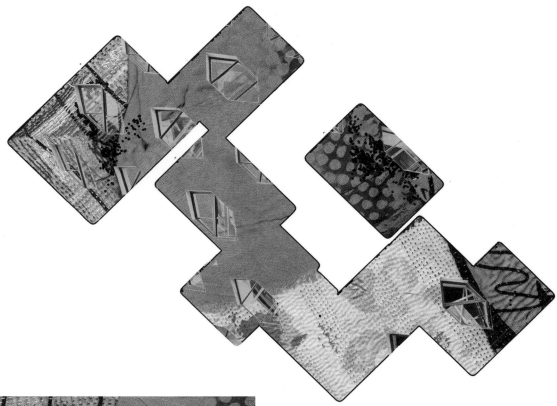

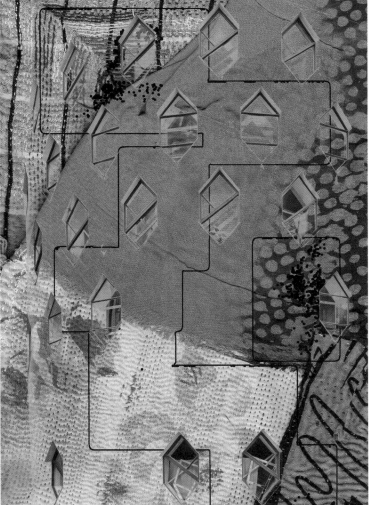

Additional Activity

Draw irregular shapes instead of a neat grid and see the effect that has on your composition.

Yayoi Kusama

Repeat, repeat and repeat

Japanese artist Yayoi Kusama uses drawing to understand the world around her. Her very personal responses to people, faces, nature and everyday objects are part of a visual universe she has drawn ever since she was a child, repeating these motifs in her work helps her to cope with complex feelings such as being one among many. In this meditative drawing activity she invites you to create and explore your own inner worlds. Empty your mind and connect with your feelings as you do it.

You will need:

Colouring pencils
or fine-tip markers
Acrylic paint
Paper or card

1
There are a lot of motifs in my art. In this painting, *The Crowd [TWXOZ]*, it is eyes. Pick your favourite single motif and draw it as many times as you can on a single page.

Why did you choose this activity?
I enjoy working with lots of different materials – from lights to mirrors, household furniture and balloons – for this I suggest marker pens and paper or acrylic paints. These are what I like to use when I am drawing or painting.

What is an artist and what do they do?
An artist is someone who creates a new world every day. I wake up early in the morning and stay up late at night just to make art in my studio. I go back to my room at night to sleep. I only rest my body so I can create something new the next day.

What made you become an artist?
My love for the world made me become an artist. Early in my life I remember being frightened and sad. My country was at war and my parents argued a lot. Making art helped me to create a brighter future. I hope that people see that my art is about love and peace. This is why I paint and I don't ever want to stop.

How would you describe your work?
Art is my way of making sense of the world. All of my works are steps on my journey.

What's fun about making art?
Making art allows me to forget my fears and anxiety. Through making art, I want to bring joy and happiness to as many people as possible. I especially love to see my works being enjoyed by young people.

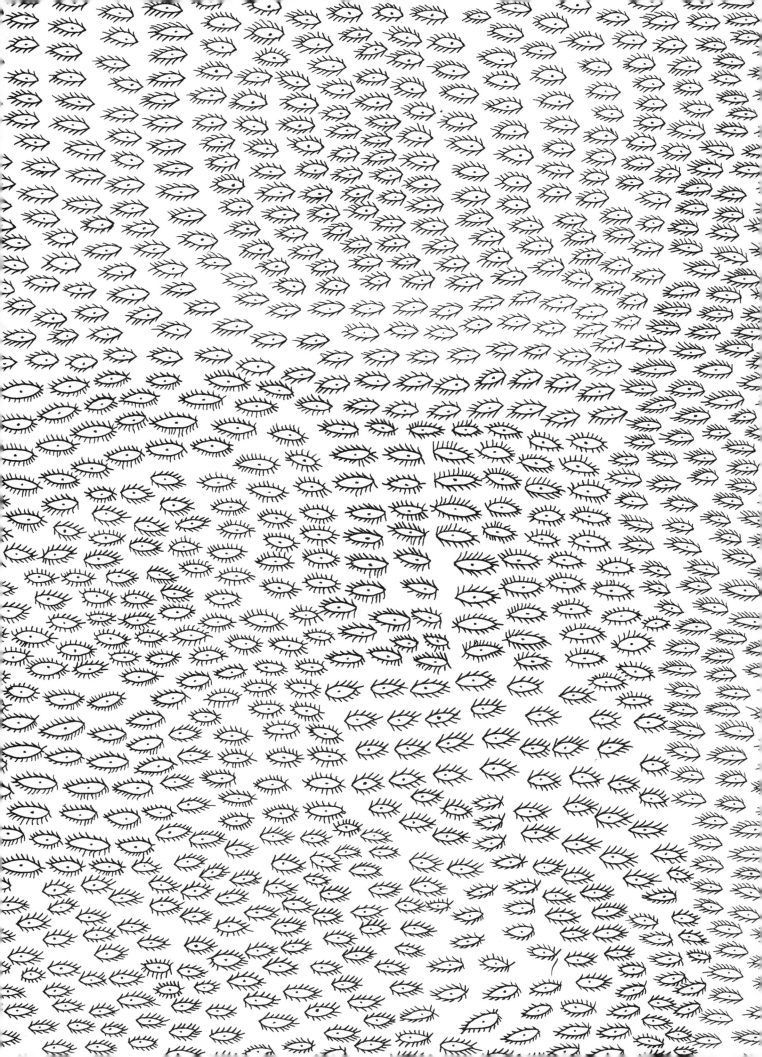

2
There are many familiar, everyday objects in my painting *Love Forever [TAOW]*, such as eyes, glasses, high heels, dogs, shoes, hats. What are your favourite things in your life? Draw them.

Artist's Note
When I was young, maybe eight or ten years old, I started to make art from my mind. I want to find out new things through my work and that was when I started to paint and draw every day.

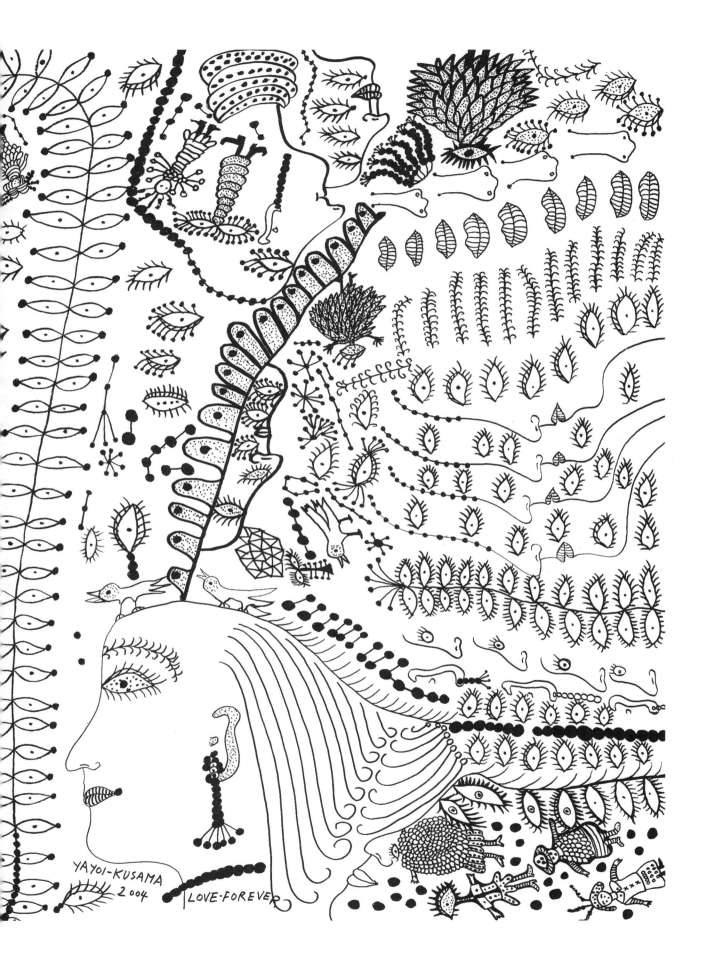

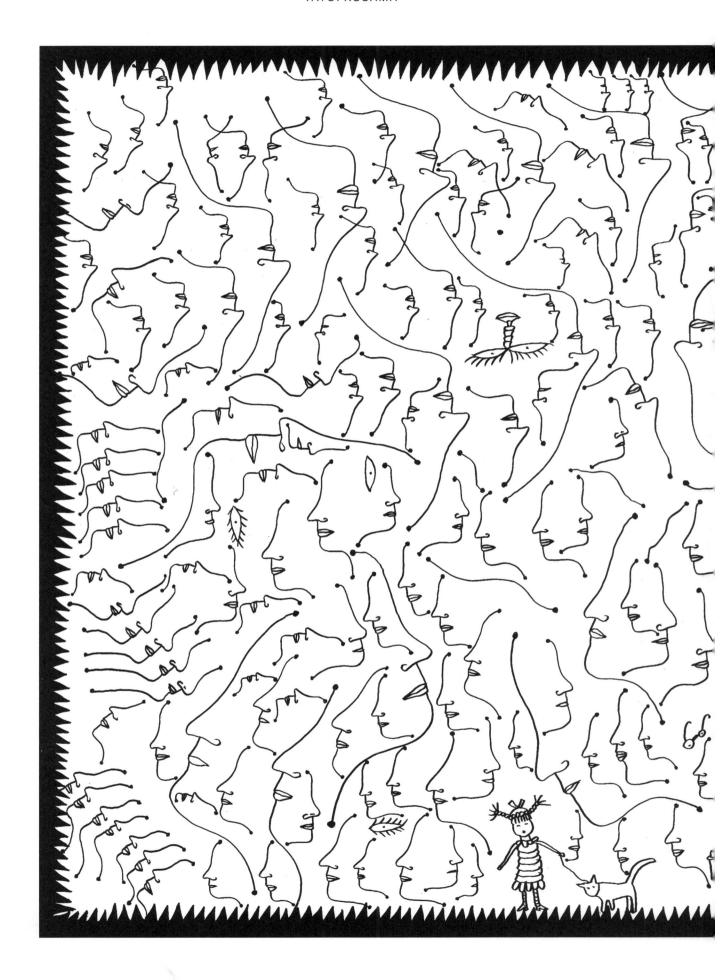

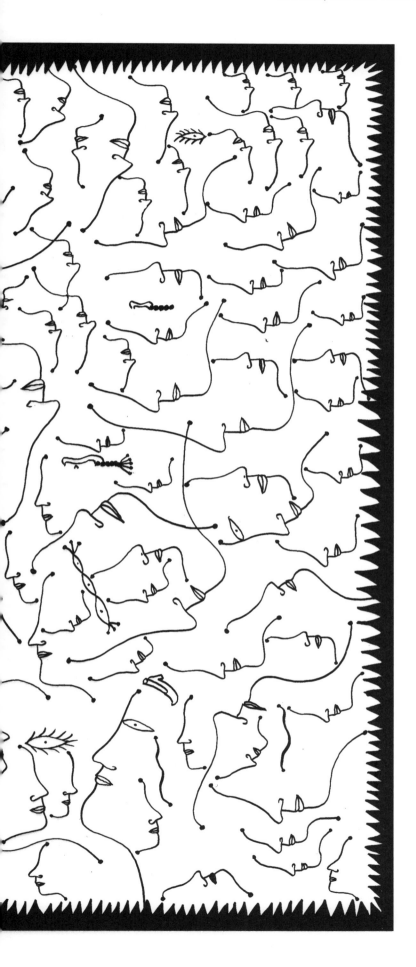

3
Look at your face carefully. What kind of lines do you see in your face? How about your friends? Everyone has different lines. Draw them. I called this painting *Lovers*.

Artist's Note

When I start to paint or draw my mind is empty. I don't know what I will do or how the painting will turn out. Each one is different. I don't think anything or prepare anything before I start. Things come from my heart or my feelings at that moment. New ideas and new visions of things I want to create are always swirling around in my head.

turn the book

5

Find your favourite landscape (or flower, tree, birds) and draw your own using polka dots and lines. Look around you wherever you are. Nature is everywhere. This painting is called *Flowering New York [OPRT]*.

4

Go outside and look at nature carefully. What kind of shapes can you find in nature? Draw the different shapes you find.

Jeremy Deller

Puzzles

Jeremy Deller was born in London and is a conceptual artist. Much of his work is collaborative and mixes humour with social and political observations. Here he gives some classic puzzle book activities a signature twist.

You will need:

Pens, pencil or fine-tip markers
Black paint
Paintbrush
Copier, scanner or printer

Why did you choose this activity?
I actually chose four activities because I wanted more pages than any of the other artists.

What is an artist and what do they do?
An artist does what they like until someone tells them off.

What made you become an artist?
The absolute and profound inability to do anything else.

How would you describe your work?
Terrible and brilliant.

What's fun about making art?
Doing this book (sort of).

Painting by Number

Kazimir Malevich, *Black Square*, 1915

1 – Black

Make your own Protest

Join the Dots

Spot the

Monaco

1.
....

2.
....

3.
....

4.
....

5.
....

Difference

Kibera, Nairobi, Kenya

1. ....

2. ....

3. ....

4. ....

5. ....

See back of book for helpful facts and figures

Michael Craig-Martin

Colour your perception

Michael Craig-Martin is an Irish conceptual artist and painter based in the UK. He is acclaimed for his bold palette and deceptively simple depictions of everyday objects. The challenge in this activity is not only filling in his line drawings, but also to think about the subjects he has selected. Try using different colour combinations and see how they change what you see.

You will need:

Copier, scanner or printer
Colouring pencils, fine-tip markers or paint
Paper or card

1
Make multiple copies of the line drawings on the following pages.

2
Colour in the drawings using any colours you want.

Why did you choose this activity?
I decided to present the same image as a simple line drawing without colour and in full colour. Anyone can see the impact the colour has and how much colour alters our perception, feeling for and understanding of the objects depicted. I also wanted to encourage others to try their hand at adding colour.

What is an artist and what do they do?
To me an artist is essentially an observer more than a creator. Architects and designers 'create' the look of the contemporary world. Artists reflect on it, notice things others have missed, find unseen references and patterns, new ways of looking, and through their work enable others to see as they do. Artists make the world we inhabit visible to us as we live it.

What made you become an artist?
Ever since I was a child I have always been excited by the visual world that we create: the world of art, architecture, cinema and design. I am driven by the need to make the things I want to see. The only role I ever wanted for myself was to be an artist.

How would you describe your work?
I have tried to explore what I see as the most basic questions in art, particularly those arising from 2D image making. I have discovered that the more basic and simple I have tried to make my work, the more complex it seems.

What's fun about making art?
The greatest pleasure is seeing what I've got when I make something. Sometimes it's a surprise, occasionally a revelation.

60

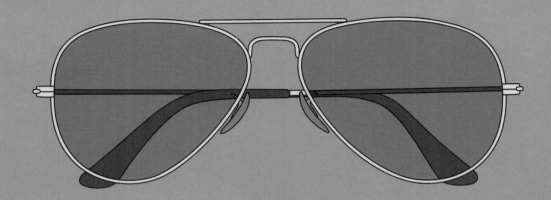

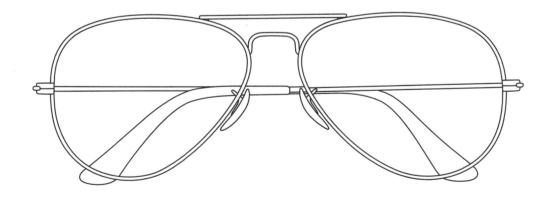

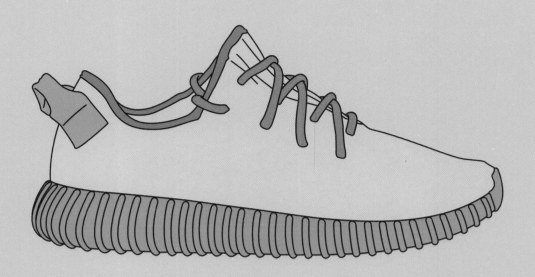

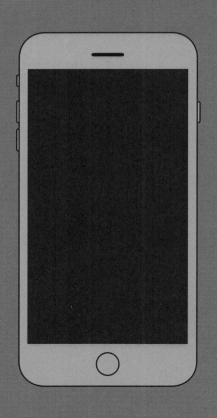

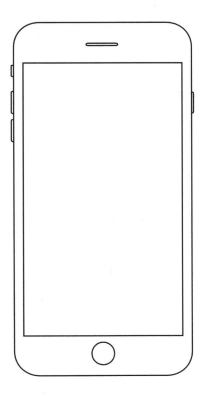

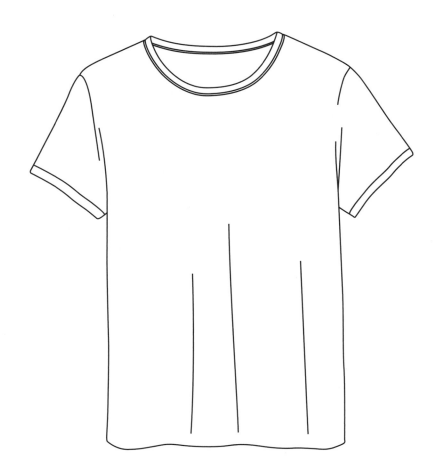

Rose Wylie

Remember, but don't remember

British artist Rose Wylie's paintings are anarchic and unruly. She delights in combining memories and imagination. In this activity she challenges you to draw everything you can remember about a scene. Wylie wants to show us that art can be very personal and we can use it to express particular recollections and emotions. Try it with friends. Can you recognise each other's versions of the same thing?

You will need:

Paper (can be anything, scraps of paper, old envelopes)
Colouring pencils
or fine-tip markers

1

For this activity, I would like you to draw from memory. It could be something from your everyday life. Or it can be a scene from a film or book. Try to remember everything connected to it and draw it without worrying about 'rightness' or 'composition' or 'order'.

Why did you choose these activities?
In art you can either respond to the world as it is, to document it, or you can use art to escape the everyday. Drawing from memory gives things another life. It's also fun and you can play for hours.

What is an artist and what do they do?
Artists usually record and, in some way, convey what they feel about what they see or the ideas which they sense are being provoked by what they are looking at.

What made you become an artist?
No particular thing. It's something I always wanted to do.

How would you describe your work?
Traditional painting and drawing, but contemporary in attitude. I work with ideas of a 'likeness' through invention or transformation – and as directly as I can. I like to allow connections to jump in which are not obviously there and to use fragments of images or ideas.

What's fun about making art?
You can work by yourself with just a pencil or pen. And nobody tells you what to do or how to do it. There are always lots of possibilities. And there are no mistakes. I don't like perfection. I think you are much happier if you can allow for imperfection.

My first example was inspired by the film *Snow White and the Seven Dwarfs*, and it was the elusive memory of the multi-coloured circular carpet that triggered 'the idea' and the extended drawing from it. The numbers and titles are included to clarify the individual drawings. The musical notes stand in for Snow White's song, *Whistle While You Work*.

Additional Activity

My second example (on pages 68–9) shows drawings I made after a journey. Try it for yourself.

I like to sit on trains and see the surroundings go past and to watch people. Someone's clothes might interest me. Or a nose. Their hair. I am responding to what I've seen but something about it will also spark my imagination.

pale red hair,
¾ coat, belted, blac
ng arched back, dark green, dipping, flutc
ngton LONDON WOMAN, fix
& lovely spotted whal

Ryan Gander
What does a label mean?

Ryan Gander is a British conceptual artist who likes to examine how language, things and meaning intersect. In this seemingly simple game, he challenges you to explore how words shape the way we relate to our surroundings.

You will need:

Paper or card
Pen or pencil
Scissors
Hole punch
String

Optional: copier

1
Copy the labels on the following pages, cut them out and punch holes in them.

2
Tie a piece of string to each label.

3
Search for items corresponding to each description. Attach the labels to them.

4
See how many additional characteristics you can come up with for each item. Make your own labels to add to the object.

Why did you choose this activity?
I am interested in the way some words represent multiple ideas and meanings. When we think about the different qualities relating to objects, we can think about them in very literal ways or more interesting, abstract ones.

What is an artist and what do they do?
Artists are people who show us things that are already there but present them in ways that we might not have considered – a bit like using a colour to underline something.

What made you become an artist?
Mobility – I knew if I was an artist I could do a different thing every day.

How would you describe your work?
I try not to describe it because visual art should be interpreted not explained. The beauty of art is that it's transformative and means different things to different people, depending on who is engaging with it.

What's fun about making art?
Making art means you can learn new things every day and be introduced to new worlds.

Something in reverse

Something sticky

Something monochrome

Something alive

Something that tessellates

Something from a collection

Something that is always on top

Something difficult

Something that can be unzipped

Something with electricity inside it

Something with a spell cast on it

Something secret

Something in a reflection

Something lucky

Something on its side

Something dirty

Something broken

Something on the periphery

71

Something that can be a mould

Something hidden

Something in order

Something slow

Something public

Something open

Something that can be a tool

Something to illuminate

Something with a beat

Something long

Something permanent

Something that grows

Something hanging

Something foreign

Something hand-made

Something to put things in

Something white

Something you don't know the use of

Something to make marks

Something dusty

Something addictive

Something that runs out

Something cosy

Something spherical

Something hard

Something empty

Something that is not mine

Something folded

Something that air flows through

Something expensive

Something older than me

Something beginning with a 'T'

Something that emits sound

Something to make you better

Something from the future

Something free

Pedro Reyes

Playtime

Pedro Reyes is a political artist from Mexico. He likes to explore the power of individuals and groups to encourage change through creativity and humour. The games he has suggested here involve two or more people working together.

Bang!

You will need:

Two or more players
Balloons

This is a game where players are pitted against one another. Each person faces their partner and a balloon is placed between them. The first or the fastest pair to break the balloon by sheer body pressure wins.

Why did you choose these activities?
Television and computers have made us sedentary, passive recipients that stare at screens. I find that a bit sad, to be honest. I wanted to revive street games, which have been around for centuries but are now are rarely played.

What is an artist and what do they do?
To be free, you need room to play, and only if you have a good amount of play in your life, are you free. An artist seizes the opportunity to invent and incorporate play into life. To reinvent life, that's what an artist does.

What made you become an artist?
I like to make things that don't exist in the world, or maybe they exist but I like them to be slightly different. In art, there is no single definition of what art is. Every artist has to bring to the table their own definition of what art means, and that's the most fun part of it.

How would you describe your work?
I do sculptures. But sculpture for me is a very broad term, it may mean crafting an object or an activity, relationships between people can also have a specific shape. Sculptures give shape to things, I am interested in form, and form may lead to meaning. I don't want to illustrate a given meaning, I want to create a form and then you may tell me what it means. Do first, theorise after.

What's fun about making art?
Art is serious fun. Some people think that art is useless, it is precisely in its uselessness that its use lies. Art is food for the soul, without art, life is dull and lame.

THIS IS A GAME WHERE LITERALLY PLAYERS ARE PITTED AGAINST ONE ANOTHER BY VERY DELIBERATELY BRINGING THEIR BODIES INTO PAIRS IN WHICH CASE THEIR EFFORTS MUST BE TIMED. EACH PERSON FACES THEIR PARTNER AND A BALLOON IS PLACED BETWEEN THEM THE FIRST OR FASTEST PAIR TO BREAK THE BALLOON BY BODY PRESSURE IS THE WINNER

Feather fun

You will need:

Feather
Sheet

Players kneel in a circle, and hold a sheet out flat by its edges. A single feather is placed in the middle of the sheet, and they all begin to blow at it. Avoid being touched by the feather, by blowing it away from your body.

Slow-Motion Fight

You will need:

Two players

Two players perform a slow-motion fight. Friends and family are invited to participate by cheering and engaging the combatants so that they feel comfortable exploring a wide range of emotions.

Minefield

You will need:

Blindfold
A selection of
non-breakable objects

1
Scatter objects through the floor of a room or go outside and place several obstacles on the ground.

2
Blindfold your partner and position them on the other side of the imaginary minefield. The object of the game is to guide your partner safely to the other side using only your voice.

3
It is key to the exercise to keep your voice calm and inform your partner about any obstacles well before she or he reaches them.

4
Do not allow your partner to stumble or fall because you were not thorough enough with your instructions.

5
When the exercise is over, trade places and re-position the obstacles so that each of you gets a turn to guide and be guided.

IS TO GUIDE YOU

THE OBJECT OF THE GAME

BY USING

IT IS KEY

PARTNER

ONLY YOUR VOICE

SAFELY

TO THE EXERCISE

THE OTHER SIDE

TO KEEP YOUR

VOICE CALM

AND

INSTRUCT YOUR PARTNER

ABOUT

SH

THM

ANY OBSTACLES

WELL BEFORE OR HE REACHES

ALLOW

DO NOT

WITH YOUR INSTRUCTIONS

BECAUSE YOU WERE NOT

THOROUGH

PARTNER

YOUR

TO STUMBLE OR FALL

ENOUGH

WHEN THE

EXERCISE

SO THAT EACH OF YOU

GETS A TURN

IS OVER

PLACES

AND RE-POSITION

OBSTACLES

YOU CAN TRADE

TO GUIDE AND BE GUIDED

Mirroring

Mirroring

You will need:

Two players but ideally more and another person to call 'Switch'.

1

In pairs, the follower and the leader stand facing and looking at each other.

2

Leader: use movements and facial expressions to project feelings onto your partner. Move slowly and allow your partner to mimic you. Take it in turns to move slowly to allow your partner to mimic you, blurring the distinction between leader and follower.

Follower: be directed by the leader. Try to imagine what the leader is feeling, synchronise your body and expressions with theirs. Imagine you are fusing into one being.

3

Whenever 'Switch' is called, exchange roles without stopping.

In pairs, the Leader and Follower stand facing looking at each other Leader use movements and facial expressions to Project Feelings onto your Partner. Move slowly to allow your partner to mimic you. Blurring the distinction between Leader and Follower. Follower; be directed by the leader try to imagine what the leader is feeling. Synchronize your body and expressions with theirs. Imagine You are fusing into one being Whenever "Switch" is called, exchange roles without Stopping

Goshka Macuga

Voyage back to the future

What happens when history is given an unexpected twist? Goshka Macuga takes colouring-in to another realm with her futuristic updates of iconic engravings. By mixing traditional and new images, London-based Polish artist Macuga shows us that there are multiple ways to understand a scene and create new stories.

You will need:

Colouring pencils or fine-tip markers

Optional: Copier, scanner or printer

Artist's Note

Before you begin, take a moment to see which bits of my drawings come from the engravings and which are sci-fi ideas I have added.

Why did you choose this activity?
As a child I used to love colouring books. I wanted to share this by extending an invitation to engage in this activity. I chose to collage iconic engravings with futuristic elements to show how one can change the way history is framed and make works from museum collections live a new life. Collaging new elements into existing images opens endless possibilities. It can be a way of learning about composition as well as an exciting exercise in narrative play and storytelling.

What made you become an artist?
I was inspired by an older generation of Polish artists who I met through my father. A few of their paintings hung in my bedroom when I was a child and always captured my imagination. I like the idea of being able to create narratives that are not quite transparent, that don't tell the whole story but instead leave visual clues which invite you to make your own journey through the work.

How would you describe your work?
Before beginning to make work, I research different ideas and study the history of the institutions I exhibit at. This process is sometimes more stimulating to me than actually making things.

What's fun about making art?
Art can be a way of living and learning. Making art enables endless possibilities to exercise different parts of your identity. Rather than committing to one form of self-expression, artists can work in different mediums or even different disciplines such as music, theatre, dance, filmmaking and so on.

What is an artist and what do they do?
An artist is a creator of visual mysteries.

Clarkson Frederick Stanfield
Martello Tower (engraved by W.B. Cooke), 1836 (top)

My drawing (on pages 82–3) shifts an 1836 landscape with a disused fort to a Martian landscape. We can see people holding signs reading 'We are still Earthlings', suggesting the scene is from a time after humans have left the earth. Science-fiction is often a comment on contemporary themes. We can speculate about why they might be protesting about their connection to earth.

Joseph Michael Gandy, *Architectural composition of framed perspectives and models of designs by Sir John Soane executed from 1780 to 1815*

Sir John Soane was the architect of many important buildings in London, such as the Bank of England, he also founded an amazing museum in his home. This watercolour imagines John Soane's un-built works as models in a gallery. My update extends the visionary creations of Soane to another era, filling parts of the gallery with futuristic buildings.

Ernesto Neto
A sensory adventure

Brazilian sculptor Ernesto Neto creates large-scale sensory installations that he describes as a 'hug'. He wants his art to slow people down, so that we reconnect with our bodies and enjoy living in the moment. Here he encourages you to try three activities that help mindfulness and celebrate a childlike sense of wonder and discovery in simple actions.

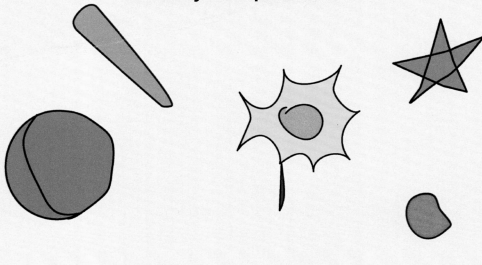

Why did you choose these activities?
It is fantastic to enjoy the sensations of the present moment. Painting a wall is a way of exercising freedom, which is especially important these days. It stimulates us to deal with materiality and gravity and encourages us to create our own environment and to care for it. There are a lot of secrets in fruit – its form, colour, smell and flavour. It is good to explore and discover. I think of fruit as sculpture. Often my sculpture is made up of cells and when you touch it you get the idea of flesh. To meditate is fun and it's a great way to calm down. To feel the wind, is good, very good. It brings us joy. If you do these activities with other people it is a great way to create and share something together.

What is an artist and what do they do?
The artist is the one who has their heart connected to the sky, the earth and the people, who blows the invisible with their fingers, brings visibility to the invisible; and plays, keeping alive the child that lives inside each one of us.

What made you become an artist?
It was by chance, perhaps the inability to become an astronaut.

How would you describe your work?
My work is a hug.

What's fun about making art?
Being a child forever. The fun thing about art is that it is everywhere, all the time – as long as we are open to it.

let's paint, the sun light

let's paint the wall?
let's paint the wall, wall
is my home, wall is my
home, sun, bird, turtle,
stone, a bee, a star
moon... sea, my friend
paint with me, paint
and repaint the wall,
of my room, a monster
a tree, they are always
with me

Paint a wall

1 Choose a wall to paint. In your bedroom, for example. Make sure you get permission if needed. You can paint it on your own or with family or friends.

2 Spread newspaper on the floor to keep it clean. Wear old clothes you don't mind getting messy.

3 Wipe your wall with a damp cloth to clean it. Let it dry.

4 Paint a coat of primer over the wall following the manufacturer's instructions. Wait for it to dry.

5 Use the eggshell paint to paint the wall a colour that will give you pleasure. Or use the eggshell paint and acrylic to paint a mural that will inspire you. If painting a mural, use the eggshell for larger areas of colour and the acrylic paints for detail.

fruit flavor

cut flavor

color fruit

dream fruit

art fruit

You will need:

A variety of fruit

Eat fruit

Eat the fruit slowly. Take care to enjoy the fruit's form, its colour, texture, smell and flavour.

dry the seeds,
under the sun

when we
cut the fruit
we discover,
landscape on it,
where spaceships can fly,
cut to see,   look... to dive fruit,
dig fruit, sea swimming into the
fruit. eating different, cutting,
    finding different forms, colors,
flavor a

        eat flavor,   89

plant the seeds

humm yamiiii

bzzzzz yuo yuo silence breathing silence
sitting down with my friends
silence breathing, then air in, air out
wind in, wind out   i feel my body
i feel my friend   quiet me,
quiet us, our heart, pum pum, pum pum,
silence sing piu piu sui sui, moon many,
sim papa birds friend   pum pum   sui sui,

Mindful meditation

1   Go somewhere quiet and relaxed.
2   Sit silently and tune into the sensation of breathing, the inhale and the exhale. Pay attention to parts of your body such as the rise and fall of your chest or your nostrils. Whenever the mind starts to wander, refocus on your breathing.

Artists' biographies

Yto Barrada (b.1971, Paris, France) draws from her Moroccan heritage to make playful work about complex issues. She lives and works in New York and in Tangier where she co-founded the popular local cinema, Cinémathèque de Tanger.
See: *Palm Sign*, 2010, Tate.

Monster Chetwynd (b.1973, London, UK) is a performance artist and sculptor and, as her name suggests, she likes art to be fun. In 2018 she covered the facade of Tate Britain in enormous glowing, slimy slugs.
See: *Hermitos Children*, *the pilot episode*, 2008, Tate.

Michael Craig-Martin (b.1941, Dublin, Ireland) is a contemporary conceptual artist and painter. He is famous for his bold line drawings of consumer objects and as an influential art teacher of students including Damien Hirst and Sarah Lucas. See: *Knowing*, 1996, Tate.

Shezad Dawood (b.1974, London, UK) makes art that is often a critical examination of identity. He draws on his British and Pakistani roots as well as modern European and American culture to create beautiful multimedia works. See: *Towards the Centre, Once More,* 2014, Tate.

Jeremy Deller (b.1966, London, UK) is unusual in that he is a winner of the Turner Prize but didn't go to art school (he studied art history) and doesn't make things (such as paintings or sculpture). Instead, he likes to work with people to 'make things happen'. Projects include inviting brass bands to play rave music; a re-enactment of a 1984 miners' strike and an inflatable Stonehenge. See: *The History of the World*, 1997–2004, Tate.

Carlos Cruz-Diez (b.1923, Caracas, Venezuela) is a key figure of optical art. He has dedicated his life to experimenting with colour, creating hypnotic, vibrant works at every scale from small paintings to large public artwork for airports, city walkways and even a hydroelectric plant.
See: *Physichromie No. 113*, 1963, Tate.

Olafur Eliasson (b.1967, Copenhagen, Denmark) is the founder of Studio Eliasson, a multidisciplinary collective whose work focusses on social and environmental issues. In 2003 he created Tate Modern's most popular public artwork, *The Weather Project*, a huge glowing sun. In 2018, he installed 24 melting icebergs from Greenland in front of Tate Modern to raise awareness about climate change. See: *Yellow versus Purple*, 2003, Tate.

Ryan Gander (b.1976, London, UK) is a conceptual artist whose work is often made with a knowing wink (he has in fact made a work with an animatronic winking eye) and is a sharp commentary on art, culture and modern life. See: *Associative Ghost Template #2*, 2012, Tate.

Yayoi Kusama (b.1929, Matsumoto, Japan). The 'Princess of Polka Dots' is one of today's most loved artists. Her work draws from feminism, minimalism, surrealism and pop art. Famous for her bright red hair and aesthetic universe of pumpkins and polka dots, Kusama wants her art to spread joy around the world. See: *The Passing Winter*, 2005, Tate.

Linder (b.1954, Liverpool, UK) burst out of Manchester's punk scene and designed cover art for Buzzcocks. She is best known for her collage art and subversive twist on feminism. See: *Untitled*, 1976, Tate.

Goshka Macuga (b.1967, Warsaw, Poland). Meticulous research and archives are important for Macuga. Working across mediums such as woven tapestry, sculpture and collage, she creates intricate, political work. See: *Death of Marxism, Women of All Lands Unite*, 2013, Tate.

Ernesto Neto (b.1964, Rio de Janeiro, Brazil) wants us all to remain childlike in our love of art and the world, and makes interactive sensory work – often large installations with tactile or aromatic materials – that invites us to smell, see and taste it. See: *We Fishing the Time (densidades e buracos de minhoca)*, 1999, Tate.

Amalia Pica (b.1978, Neuquén, Argentina) is an artist fascinated by the methods and meanings of communication. Her work draws on her childhood in North Patagonia; she is from the first generation after a dictatorship. Pica says she is always 'looking for the possibility that joy and happiness can be a form of resistance.' See: *Venn diagrams (under the spotlight)*, 2011, Tate.

Pedro Reyes (b.1972, Mexico City, Mexico) makes political work that addresses the key social issues of our time. He is perhaps best known for his project *Palas por Pistolas (Shovels for Guns)*, in which he melted collected guns into steel and used that steel to fabricate shovels planting trees.

David Shrigley (b.1968, Cheshire, UK) is celebrated for his witty drawings and for being very tall. His art is often subversive, and at times can be disturbing. His sculpture *Really Good*, a huge bronze thumbs up with a really long thumb, sat on the Fourth plinth of London's Trafalgar Square, from 2016–18. See: *Stop It*, 2007, Tate.

Rose Wylie (b.1934, Kent, UK). Wylie emerged onto the art scene in her seventies and is one of today's most successful painters. Her studio is in her house and she paints whatever takes her fancy, from footballer Wayne Rooney to her cats, vegetables she likes and Quentin Tarantino films. See: *Lorry Art*, 2010, Tate.